Gurgles and Growls
LEARNING ABOUT YOUR STOMACH

WRITTEN BY PAMELA HILL NETTLETON
ILLUSTRATED BY BECKY SHIPE

FOUNTAINDALE PUBLIC LIBRARY DISTRICT
300 West Briarcliff Road
Bolingbrook, IL 60440-2894
(630) 759-2102

Thanks to our advisers for their expertise, research, and advice:
Angela Busch, M.D., All About Children Pediatrics, Minneapolis, Minnesota

Susan Kesselring, M.A., Literacy Educator
Rosemount-Apple Valley-Eagan (Minnesota) School District

PICTURE WINDOW BOOKS
MINNEAPOLIS, MINNESOTA

Managing Editor: Bob Temple
Creative Director: Terri Foley
Editor: Kristin Thoennes Keller
Editorial Adviser: Andrea Cascardi
Copy Editor: Laurie Kahn
Designer: Melissa Voda
Page production: The Design Lab
The illustrations in this book were rendered digitally.

Picture Window Books
5115 Excelsior Boulevard
Suite 232
Minneapolis, MN 55416
1-877-845-8392
www.picturewindowbooks.com

Printed in the United States of America.

Library of Congress Cataloging-in-Publication Data
Nettleton, Pamela Hill.
  Gurgles and growls: learning about your stomach / by Pamela Hill
Nettleton ; illustrated by Becky Shipe.
    p. cm. — (The amazing body)
Summary: An introduction to the stomach and other parts of the digestive
system and how they function.
  ISBN 1-4048-0253-3 (Reinforced Library Binding) 1. Stomach—Juvenile
literature. [1. Stomach. 2. Digestive system.] I. Shipe, Becky, 1977– ill.
II. Title.
  QP151 .N48 2004
  612.3—dc22   2003018191

Do you know where you get your energy?
From your food! But your body can't turn
food into energy without your stomach.

Yum! Pizza tastes great!
But what happens after you chew it?

When you swallow, your throat muscles push food down into your stomach. Now your stomach has a job to do!

Your stomach has muscles, too. They can stretch
to hold one, two, or three pizza slices. This
might not feel good, but your stomach can do it!

Then your stomach shrinks back down again.
Cool trick!

You can help your stomach do its job. Chew your food well and for a long time.

Your stomach squeezes and mashes up your food. Your stomach also makes juices.

Your stomach takes about three hours to break down a meal.

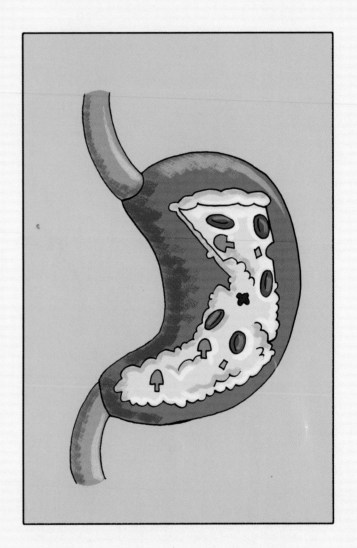

These juices mix with your food to make
it soft and mushy.

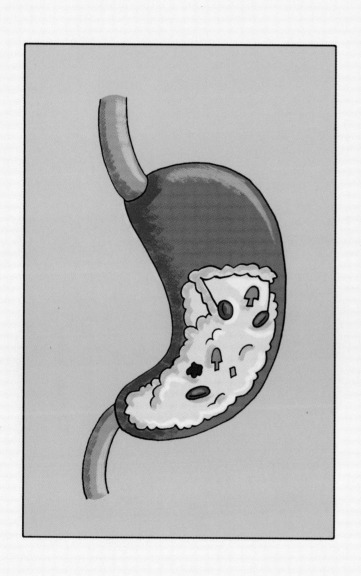
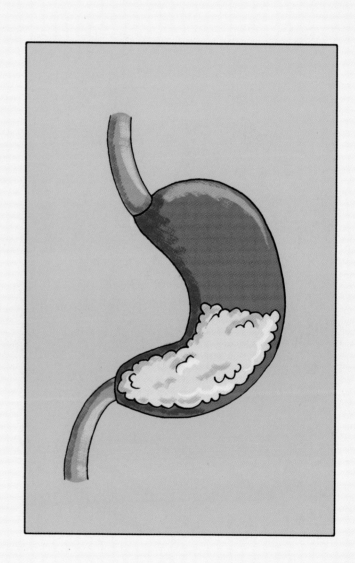

Your stomach turns food into a liquid mixture. This process gets the food ready to be turned into energy.

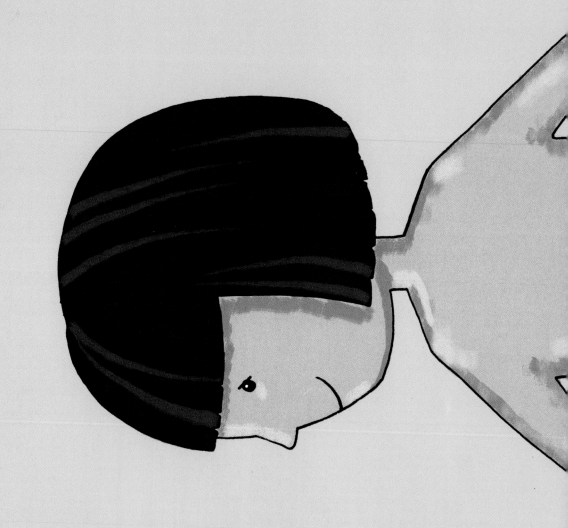

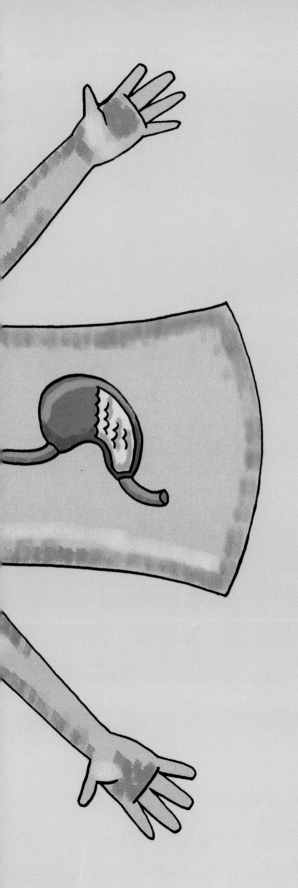

Greasy food such as fast-food hamburgers can take your stomach a long time to digest.

The process of turning food into energy is called digestion.

After your stomach digests food for a while,
it doesn't look like your lunch anymore!

Now the liquid food is ready to be pushed out of the bottom of your stomach. From there, it goes into your small intestine. That's where your body gets energy from your food.

Your small intestine is 22 feet (6.7 meters) long! That's about as tall as a two-story house!

When you go to the bathroom, your body
is getting rid of the parts of food it can't use.

Passing gas also is a normal part of digestion.

RESTROOM

When your stomach growls, it thinks it's meal time. Your stomach is getting ready to work hard.

Sometimes your stomach hurts. This might mean you ate too much or that you are sick. Sometimes people throw up, or vomit.

Your body throws up to protect you. It knows that germs have gotten into the food or into the stomach itself. Then it sends food back up and out your mouth. Throwing up does not feel good!

Feeling worried or scared can make your stomach hurt, too.

There are special doctors who take care
of stomach problems.

These doctors study the parts of the body that help digest food. The doctors also ask questions and perform tests in order to help them understand what might be wrong.

Doctors who take care of stomach problems are called gastroenterologists.

It is easy to help your stomach feel good most of the time. Drink a lot of water each day. Eat lots of fruits and vegetables. Don't eat treats or fast food very often.

Twirling in circles or riding on carnival rides can upset your stomach.

Be smart about feeding your stomach!

THE STOMACH

The food you swallow travels down a tube called your esophagus. This tube moves the food to your stomach, which turns your food into a liquid mixture. Your stomach muscles then push the mixture into the small intestine. The small intestine breaks down the food even more so your body can use it for energy.

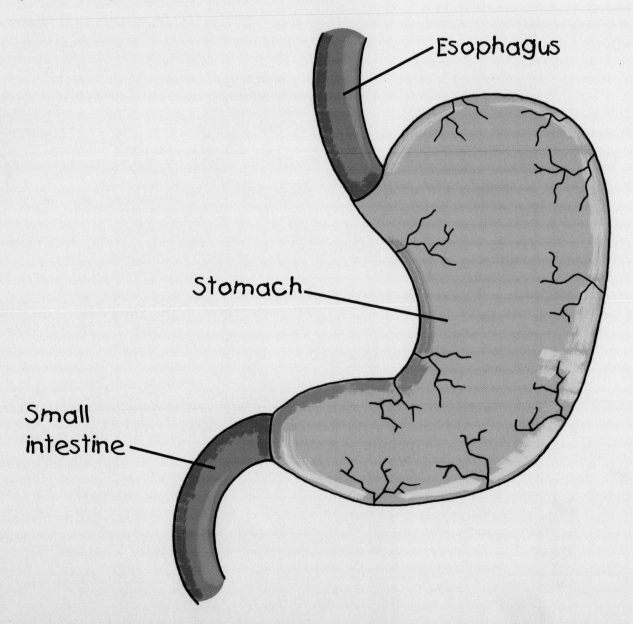

Esophagus

Stomach

Small intestine

PRETEND YOU ARE YOUR STOMACH!

Ready to eat lunch? Get a plastic food-storage bag with a top that seals. Fill it with some lunch foods. Maybe the lunch includes a sandwich, a strawberry, a slice of green pepper, a cookie, and milk. Seal the bag tightly. Now, pretend your hands are the stomach muscles! Mash it all up by squeezing the bag. Keep squeezing it until all the food is mixed together. Yuck!

TOOLS OF THE TRADE

Doctors can see inside your stomach by taking a special picture called an X-ray. Doctors don't use a camera to take this kind of picture. They use an X-ray machine. It takes pictures through your skin!

GLOSSARY

chew (CHOO)—to grind up food with your teeth

digestion (duh-JESS-chuhn)—when your body turns food into energy

gastroenterologist (GASS-troh-en-tur-awl-uh-jist)—a doctor who studies and treats problems with digestion

mouth (MOUTH)—where chewing starts your digestion

small intestine (SMAWL in-TESS-tin)—where your liquid food goes after it leaves the stomach

stomach (STUHM-uhk)—a bag of muscle that turns your food into liquid

vomit (VOM-it)—when your stomach sends liquid food back up and out your mouth

TO LEARN MORE

At the Library

Holub, Joan. *I Have a Weird Brother Who Digested a Fly*. Morton Grove, Ill.: Albert Whitman, 1999.

Showers, Paul. *What Happens to a Hamburger?* New York: HarperCollins, 2001.

Ylvisaker, Anne. *Your Stomach*. Mankato, Minn.: Bridgestone Books, 2002.

On the Web

Fact Hound offers a safe, fun way to find Web sites related to this book. All of the sites on Fact Hound have been researched by our staff.

http://www.facthound.com

1. Visit the Fact Hound home page.
2. Enter a search word related to this book, or type in this special code: 1404802533.
3. Click the FETCH IT button.

Your trusty Fact Hound will fetch the best sites for you!

INDEX